THE
#
LORD'S PRAYER

ILLUSTRATED BY *Heidi Holder*

FRONT STREET, INC.
Asheville, North Carolina

For Alexandra Elizabeth

✝

THE LORD'S PRAYER

Our
father who
art in heaven,
hallowed
be thy name.

THY
KINGDOM
COME,

Thy
WILL BE DONE,
ON EARTH AS IT
IS IN HEAVEN.

Give
US THIS DAY
OUR DAILY BREAD

And
Forgive
us our
Trespasses,

As
WE FORGIVE
THOSE WHO
TRESPASS
AGAINST US.

And
lead us not
into temptation,

But deliver us from evil.

FOR
THINE IS THE
KINGDOM, THE POWER,
AND THE GLORY
FOR EVER AND EVER.

AMEN

ACKNOWLEDGMENTS

I WISH TO THANK Dorling Kindersley Ltd. for its *Eyewitness Handbooks: Butterflies and Moths* (London, 1992), which I used as a reference for the butterflies and moths at the bottom of the lemur picture. (In some cases I changed the position of the wings and antennae, but I tried to copy these beautiful creatures as accurately as possible.) And I thank Chanticleer Press for the *National Audubon Society Field Guide to North American Insects and Spiders* (New York, 1980) and the *National Audubon Society Field Guide to North American Butterflies* (New York, 1981), which were the sources for most of the butterflies and insects in the border around the egrets, for seven of the butterflies surrounding the Lamb of God, and for two moths and a few insects in the starling picture. In addition, I am very grateful to the American Museum of Natural History for allowing me to use the museum exhibits of birds and animals as source material for some of my illustrations. Being able to see and sketch the details of the animals and birds was invaluable. I, of course, created my own backgrounds. Finally, I also want to thank Cary Sol Wolinsky for permission to use his wonderful photograph of a "half-shorn sheep" that appeared in the May 1988 issue of *National Geographic* as a model for my painting of the Lamb of God.

THE COVER

In the cover picture there is a fish, an ancient symbol of Jesus. Fearing Roman persecution, early Christians referred to Jesus in code, using the first letters of the phrase "Jesus Christ, God's Son, Saviour" in Greek. These letters spelled out the Greek word for fish, and so the picture of a fish was the coded symbol for Jesus. Also in the cover picture are iris and cyclamen flowers, symbols of the Virgin Mary.

OUR FATHER...

The swallows in the border symbolize Jesus' victory over death. These swallows build small mud nests, and when they emerge and fly heavenward they seem to enact the resurrection.

THY KINGDOM COME...

Donkeys have two narrow black lines in their fur, one going down the spine and the other crossing over the shoulders, thereby forming the shape of a cross. Many believe the donkey was blessed with this marking because Jesus chose a donkey to carry him into Jerusalem.

THY WILL BE DONE...

The animals in the picture derive from Isaiah 11:6 (The Holy Bible, New King James Version, Thomas Nelson, Inc., Nashville, 1982):

> *The wolf also shall dwell with the lamb,*
> *The leopard shall lie down with the young goat,*
> *The calf and the young lion and the fatling together;*
> *And a little child shall lead them.*

The birds perching on the border tops are goldfinches. Tradition has it that the goldfinch nests in thorns, and so the bird has become a symbol of the Passion of Jesus.

GIVE US THIS DAY...

Dogwood blossoms show the suffering of Jesus on the cross. The petals bear the markings of his head, bloodied by the crown of thorns, and the wounds in his hands and feet.

AND FORGIVE US OUR TRESPASSES...

For the borders of this picture I was inspired by a humorous remark made by the famous scientist and author J.B.S. Haldane. When asked, toward the end of his brilliant career, to give his thoughts on God and nature, he replied that, to judge by the millions and millions of insects in the world, God "seems to have an inordinate fondness for beetles."

AS WE FORGIVE THOSE...

For this picture I wanted a very gentle creature who would seem to be saying the line of the prayer. I found her at the American Museum of Natural History. She is a lemur known as *Indri indri*. These lemurs live in the treetops of the forests of Madagascar. They are monogamous and vegetarian, and when involved in territorial disputes they sing to each other rather than fight. They are, sadly, on the endangered species list. (I was unable to find any descriptions or pictures of *Indri indri* young, so I used artistic license to paint them as I imagined them to be.)

AND LEAD US NOT...

The Moluccan salmon-crested cockatoo is a very clever creature, and its curiosity—in this case it is toying with a blue crab—could lead to painfully pinched toes!

BUT DELIVER US FROM EVIL...

The deer is a symbol of man's yearning for God. The first line of Psalm 42 reads, "As the deer longs for streams of water, so my soul longs for you, O God" (New American Bible). There are many tales of deer in Christian lore. St. Eustace saw a glowing cross between the antlers of a deer. St. Hubert had a similar vision. In one common legend, St. Giles, a hermit, kept a small deer as a pet. A heathen king with his archers and hounds went hunting in the forest where St. Giles lived. Spying St. Giles's little deer, the king let fly his arrow. St. Giles rushed from the thicket and flung his arms around his beloved pet, saving its life while taking the arrow's wound himself. Immediately the king's horse knelt to the ground, and his hunting dogs, transfixed by the Holy Spirit, fell silent and did not attack. The amazed king and all his court converted to Christianity. For these and other tales, see Donald Attwater's invaluable *A Dictionary of Saints*, Penguin Books, Hazell, Watson & Viney Ltd. (Aylesbury, 1965).

FOR THINE IS THE KINGDOM...

The Lamb of God is surrounded by butterflies, which traditionally symbolize the resurrection of all humankind.

The text follows the 1928 edition of the Book of Common Prayer.
Illustrations copyright © 2004 by Heidi Holder
Printed in China
DESIGN Evansday Design
All rights reserved
FIRST EDITION